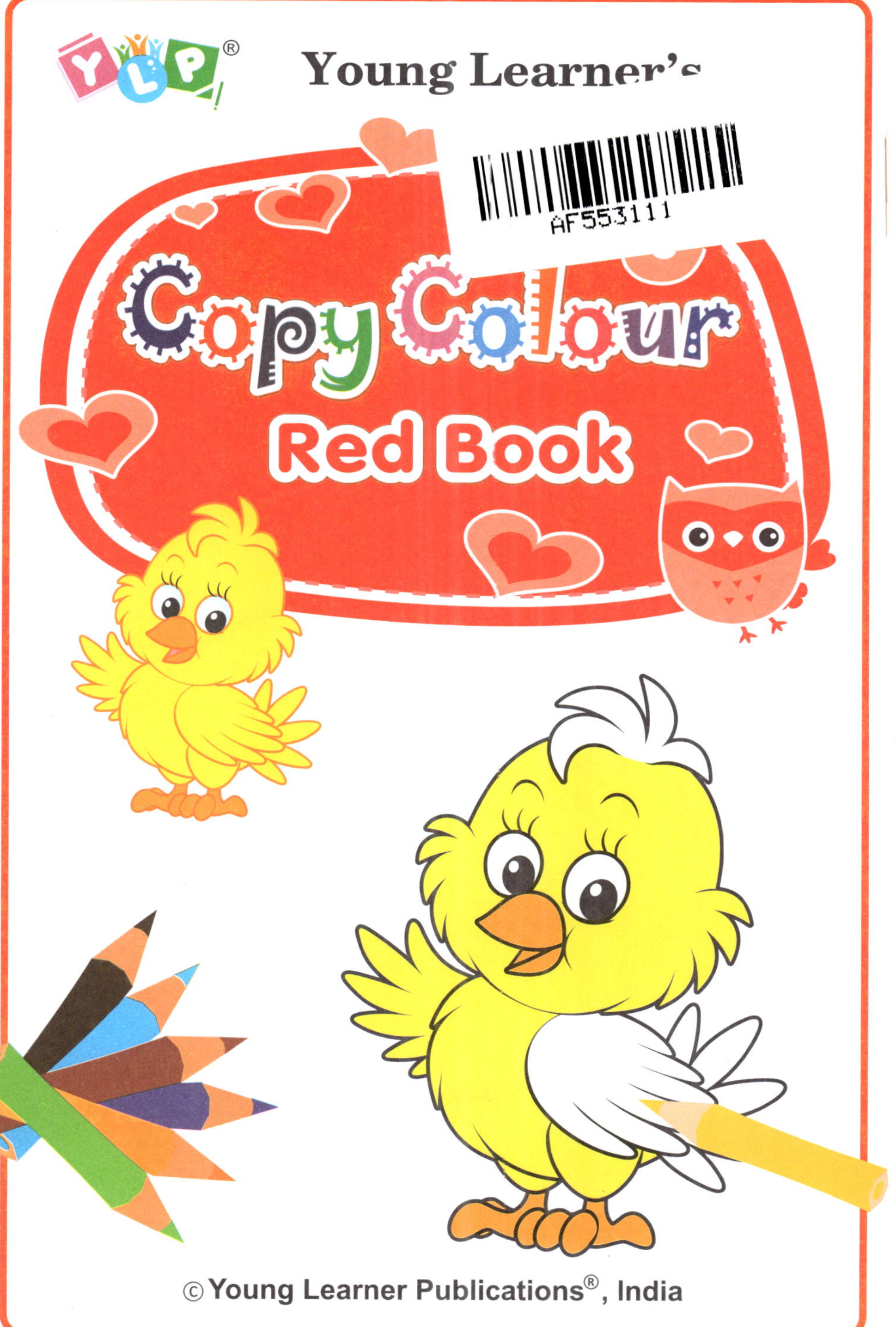
YLP
Young Learner's
AF553111
Copy Colour
Red Book

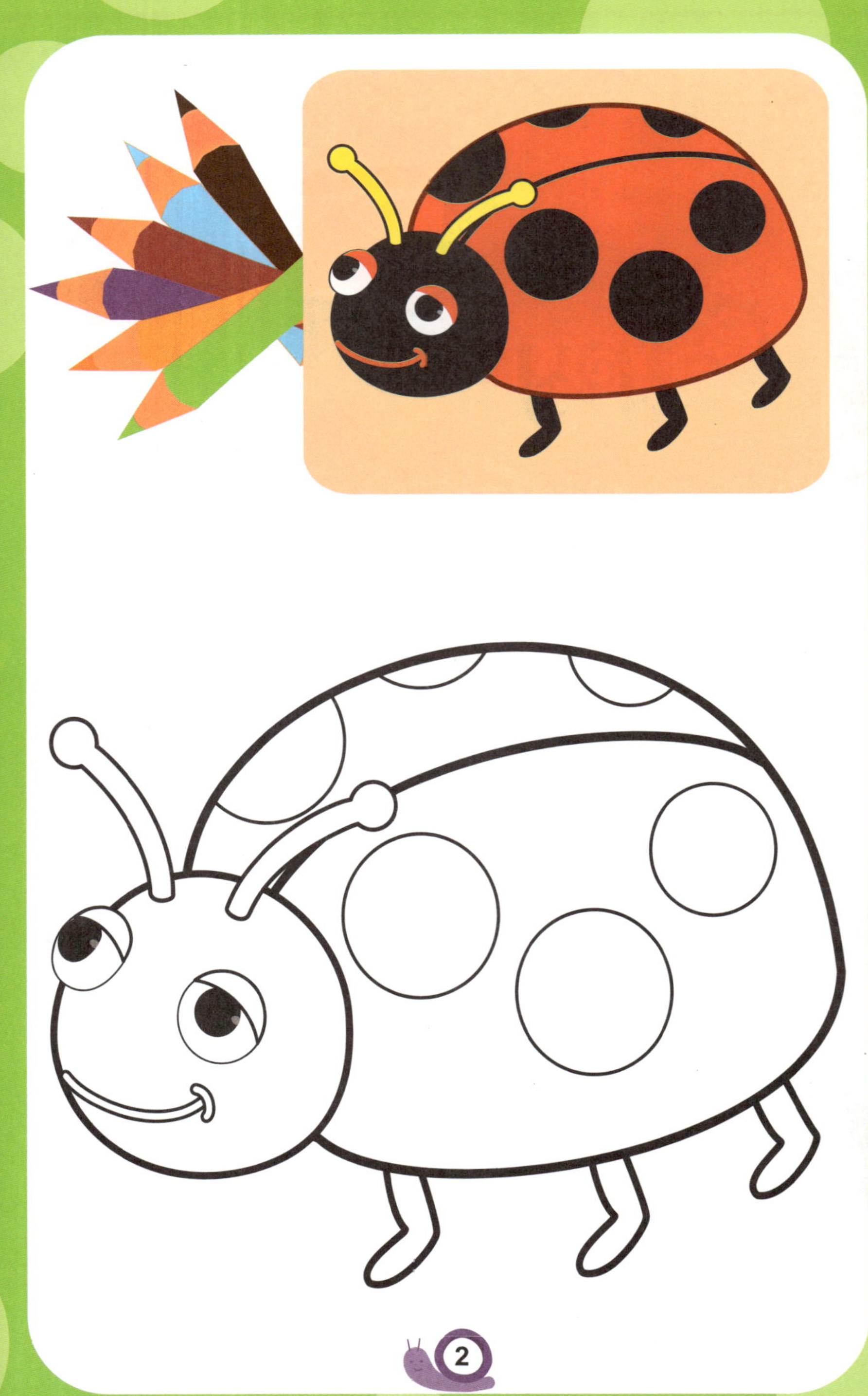

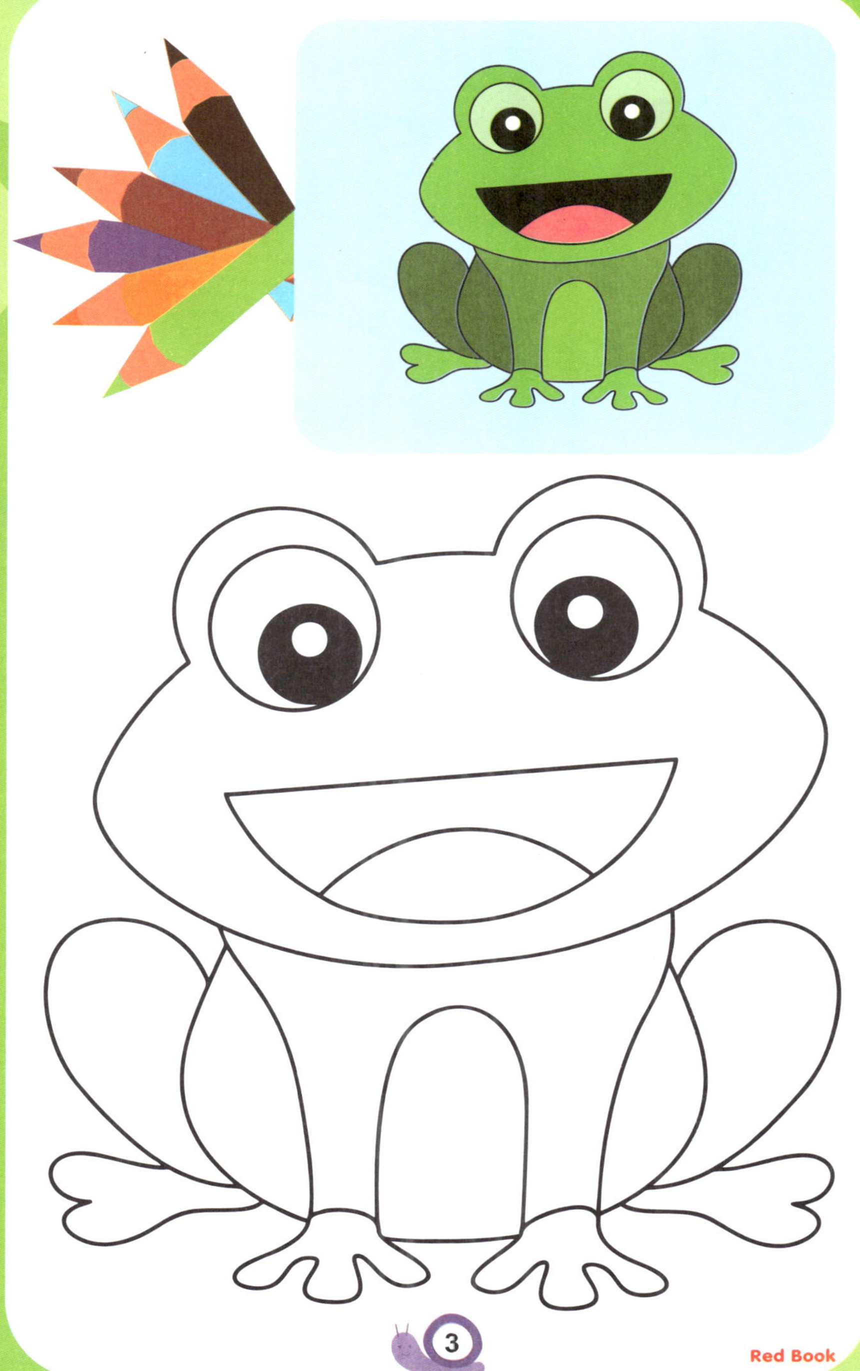

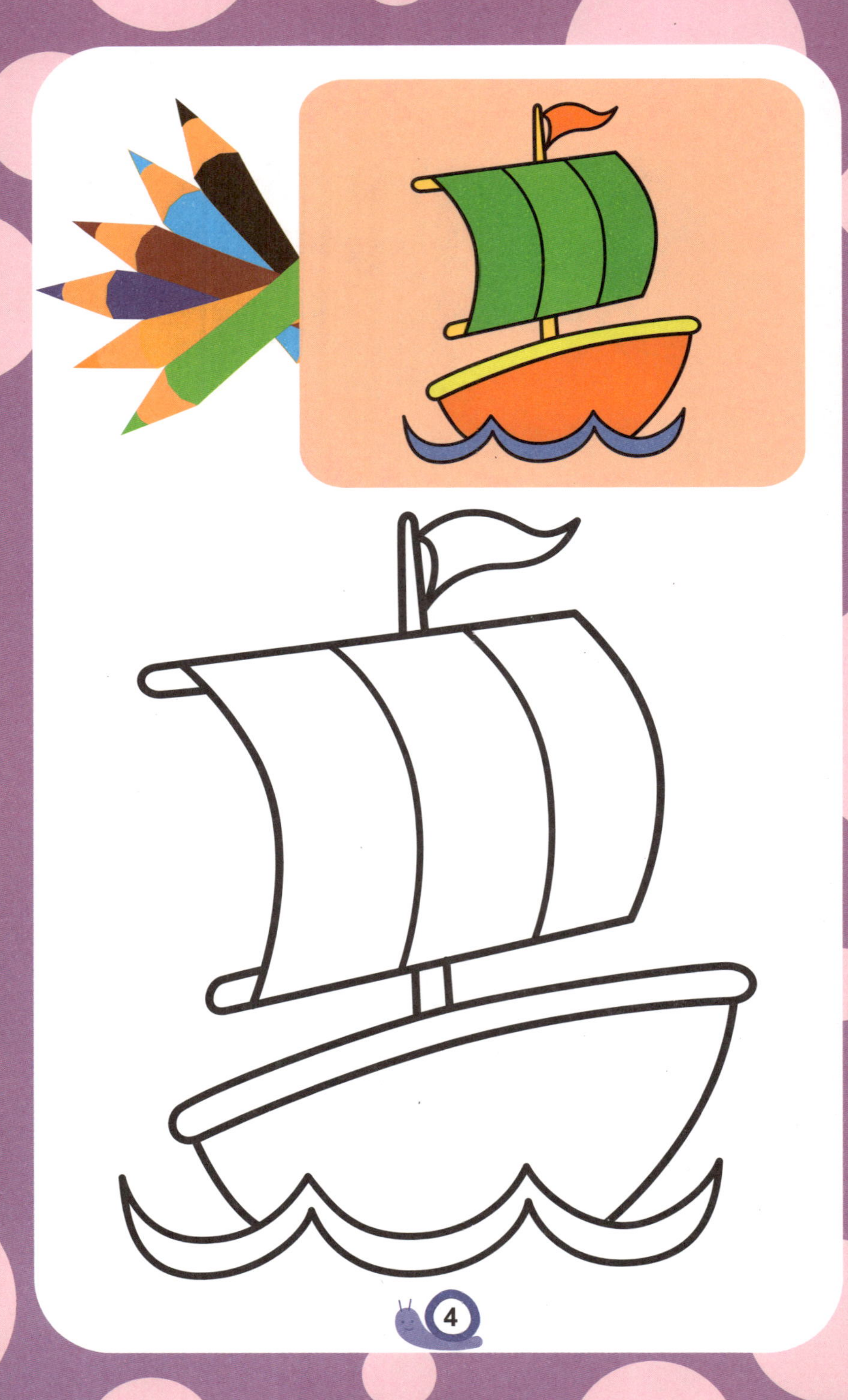

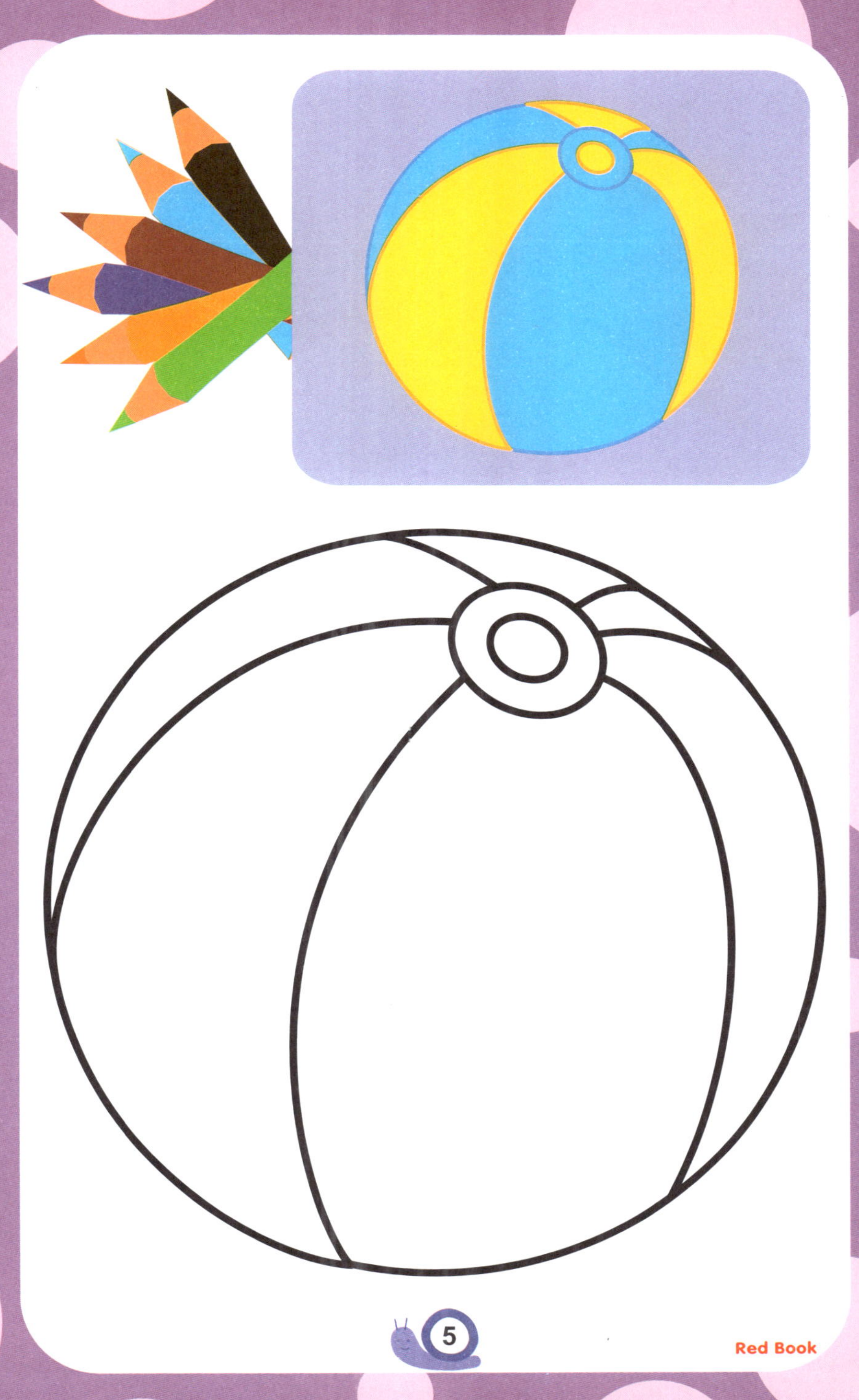

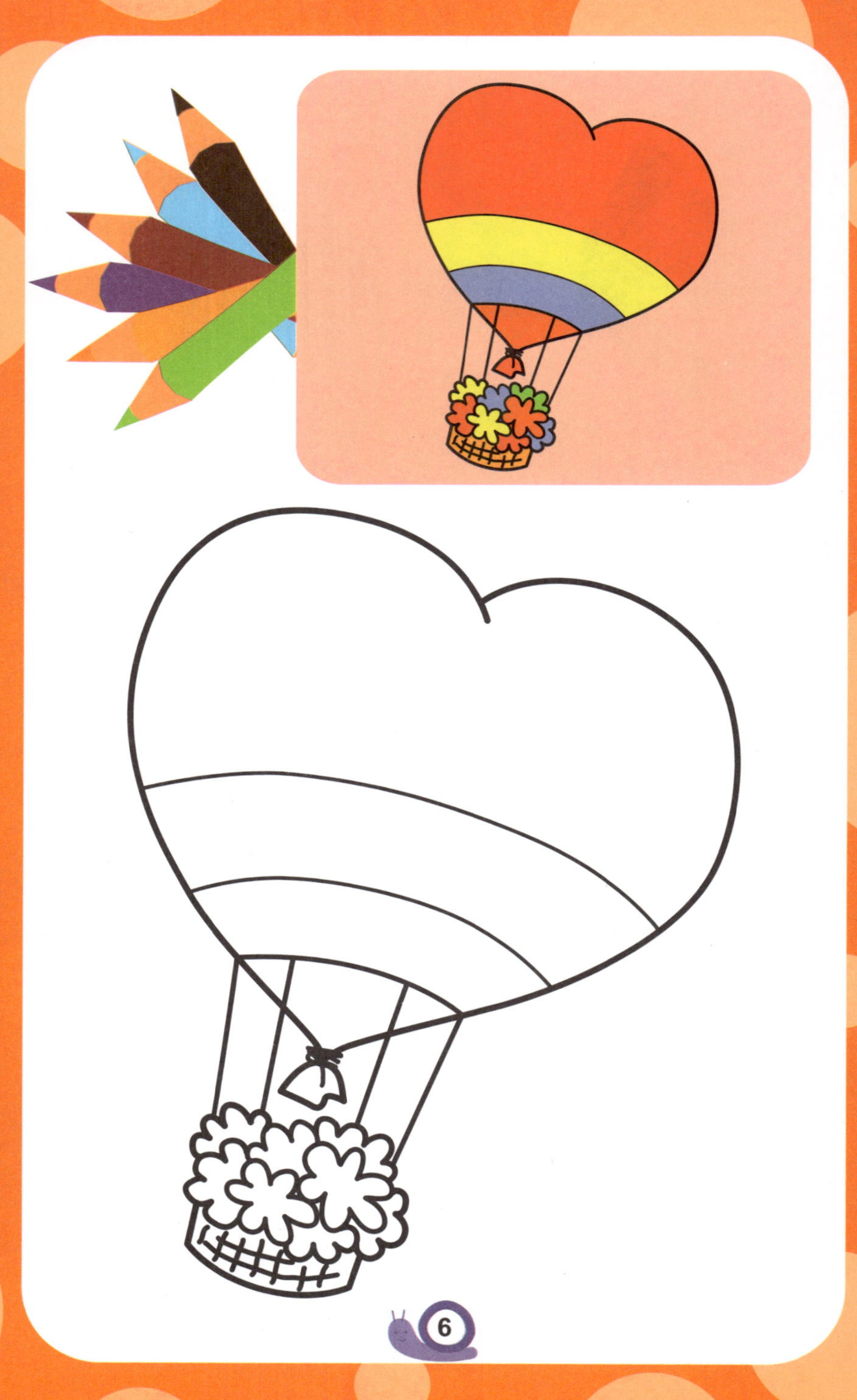

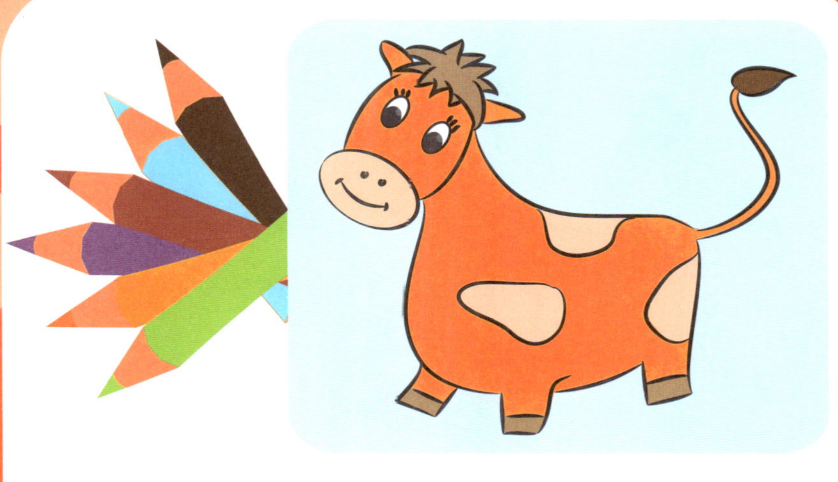

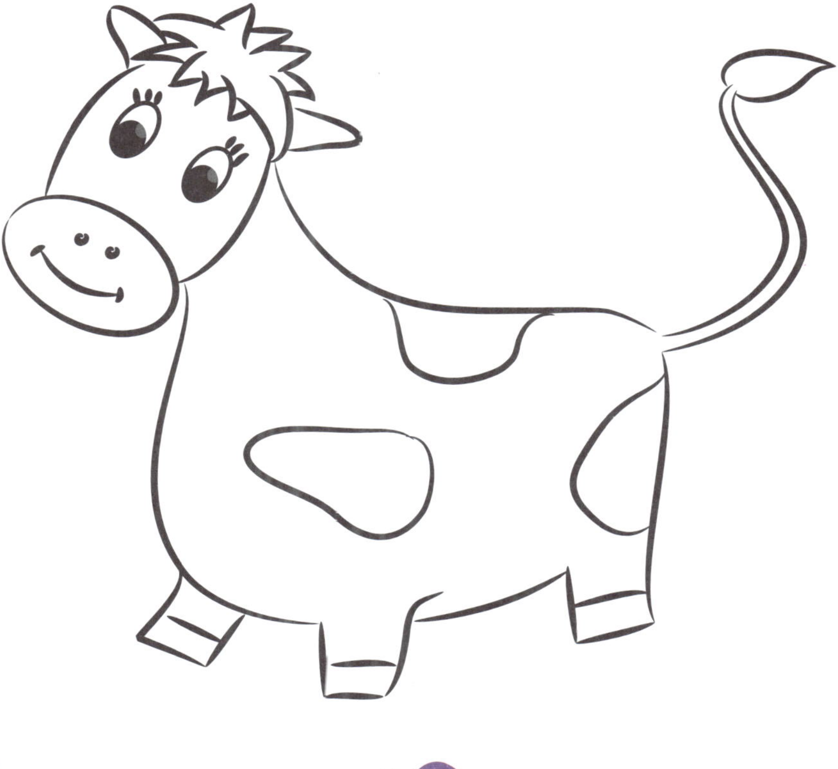

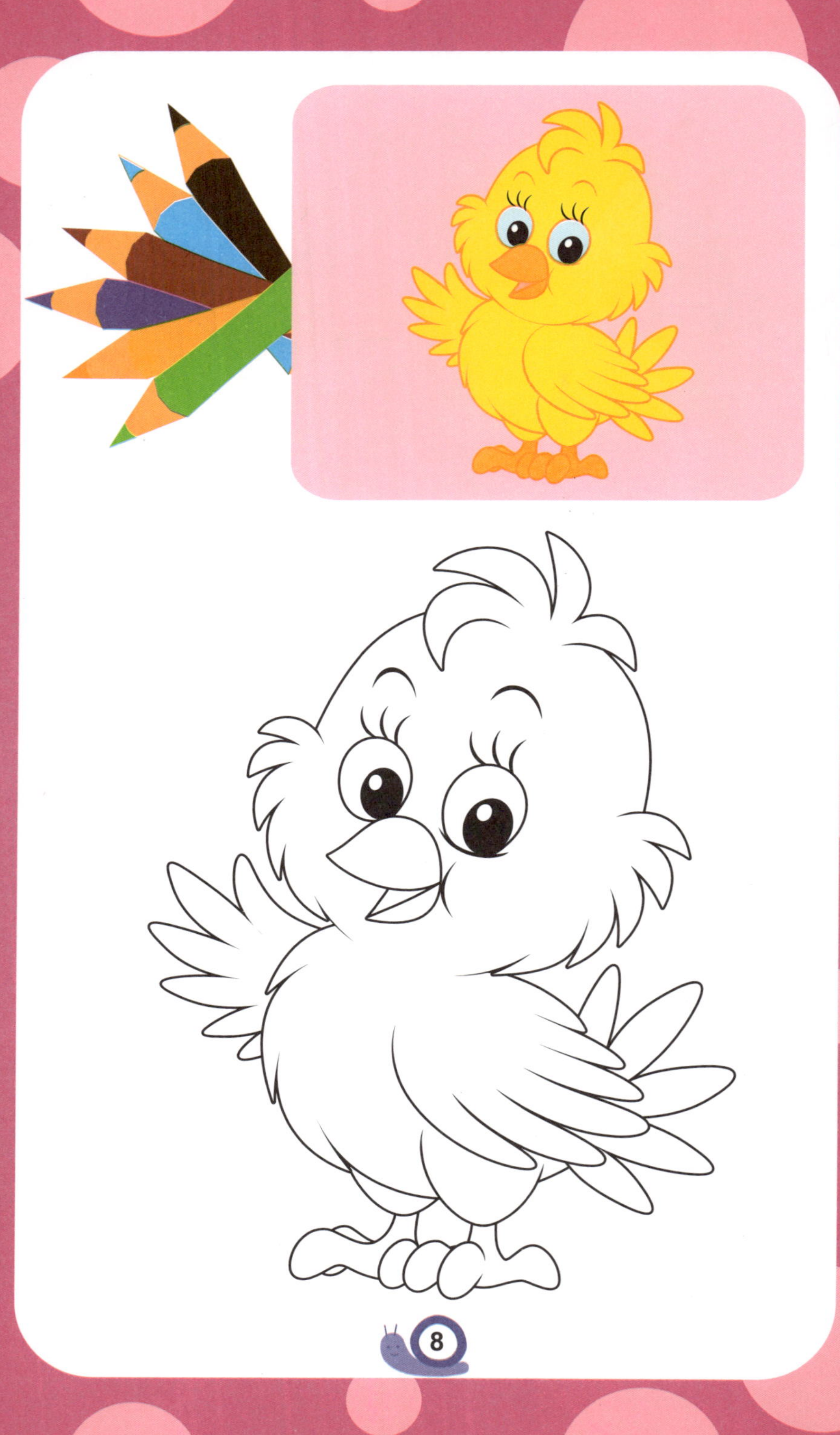

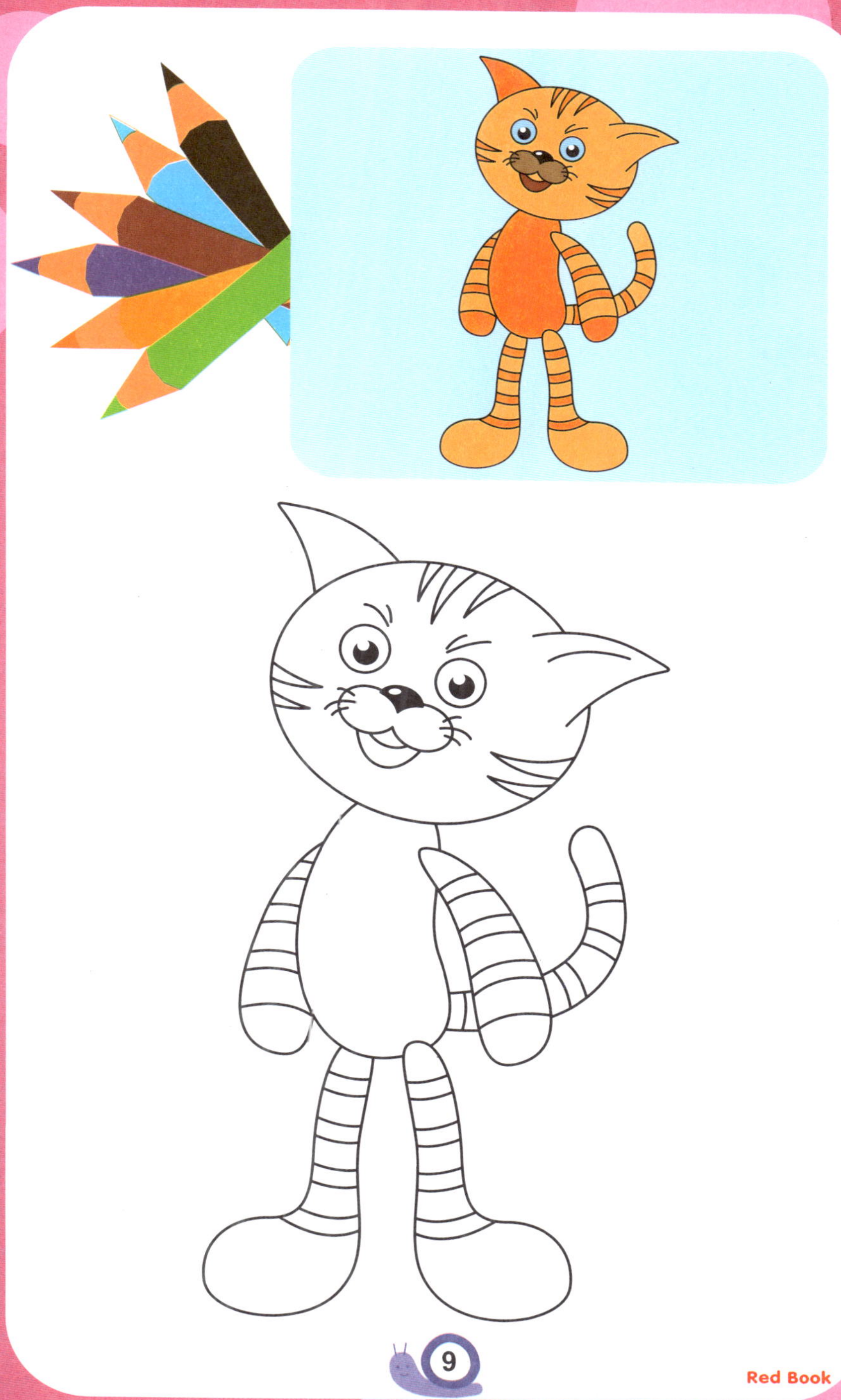

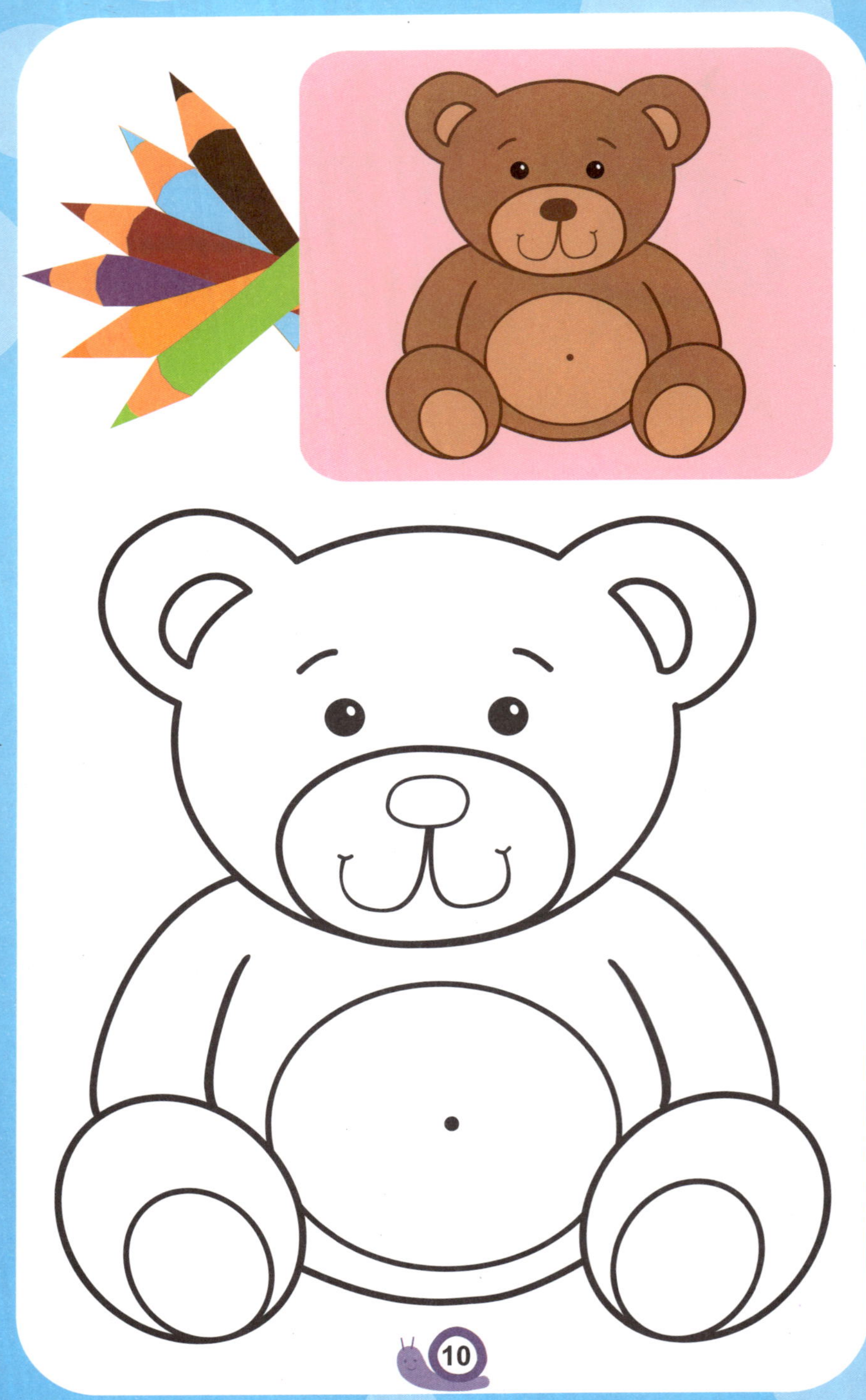

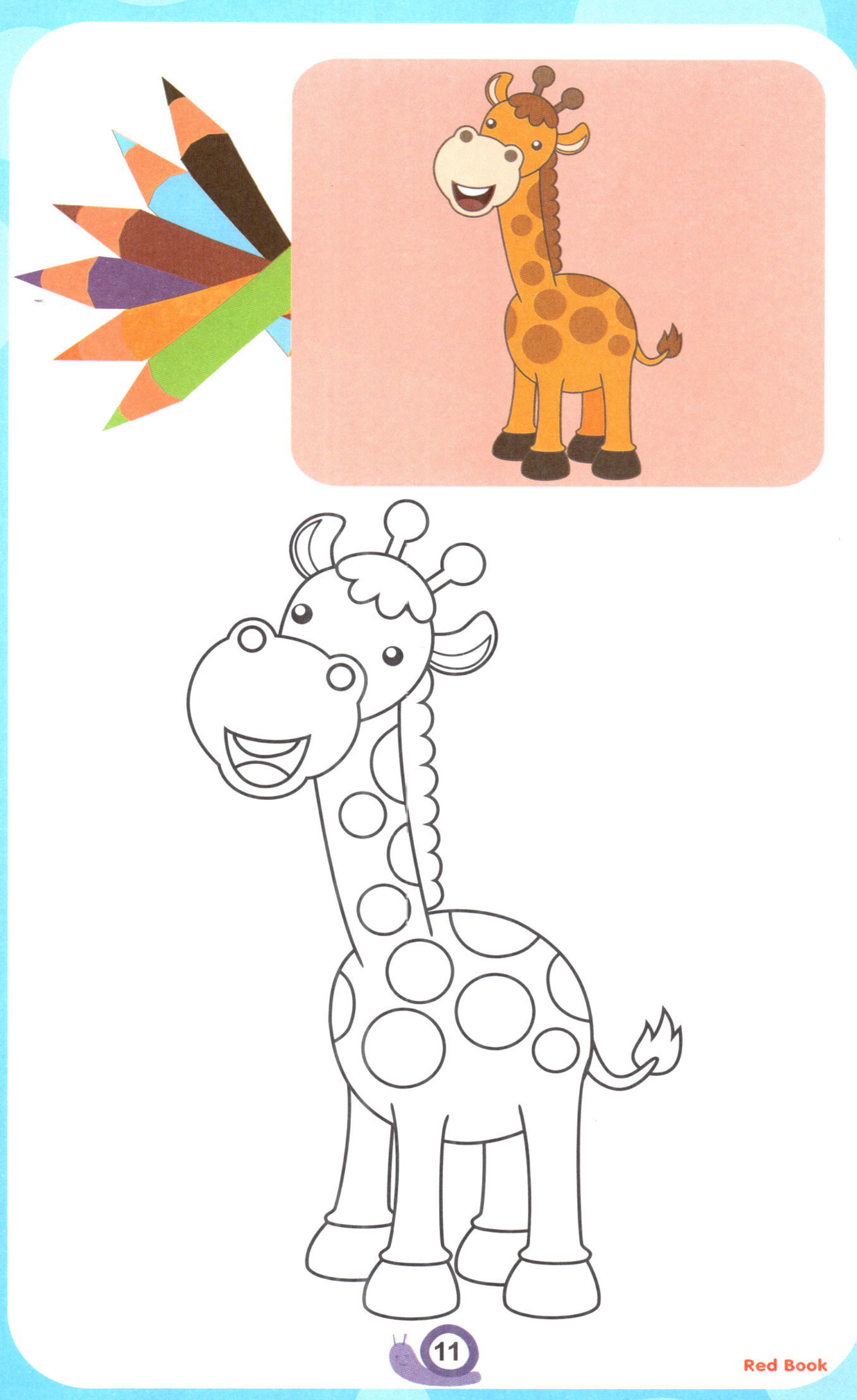

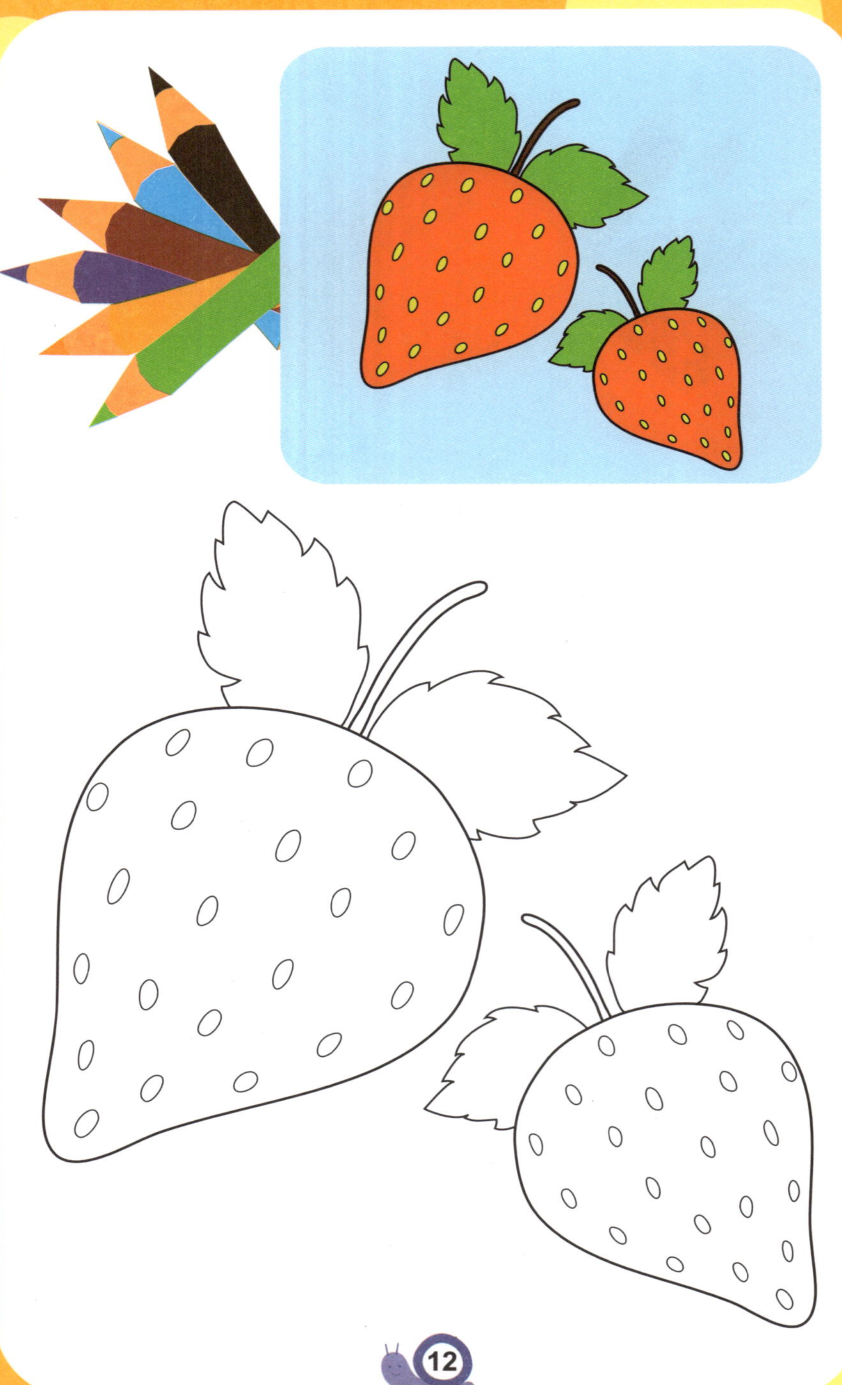

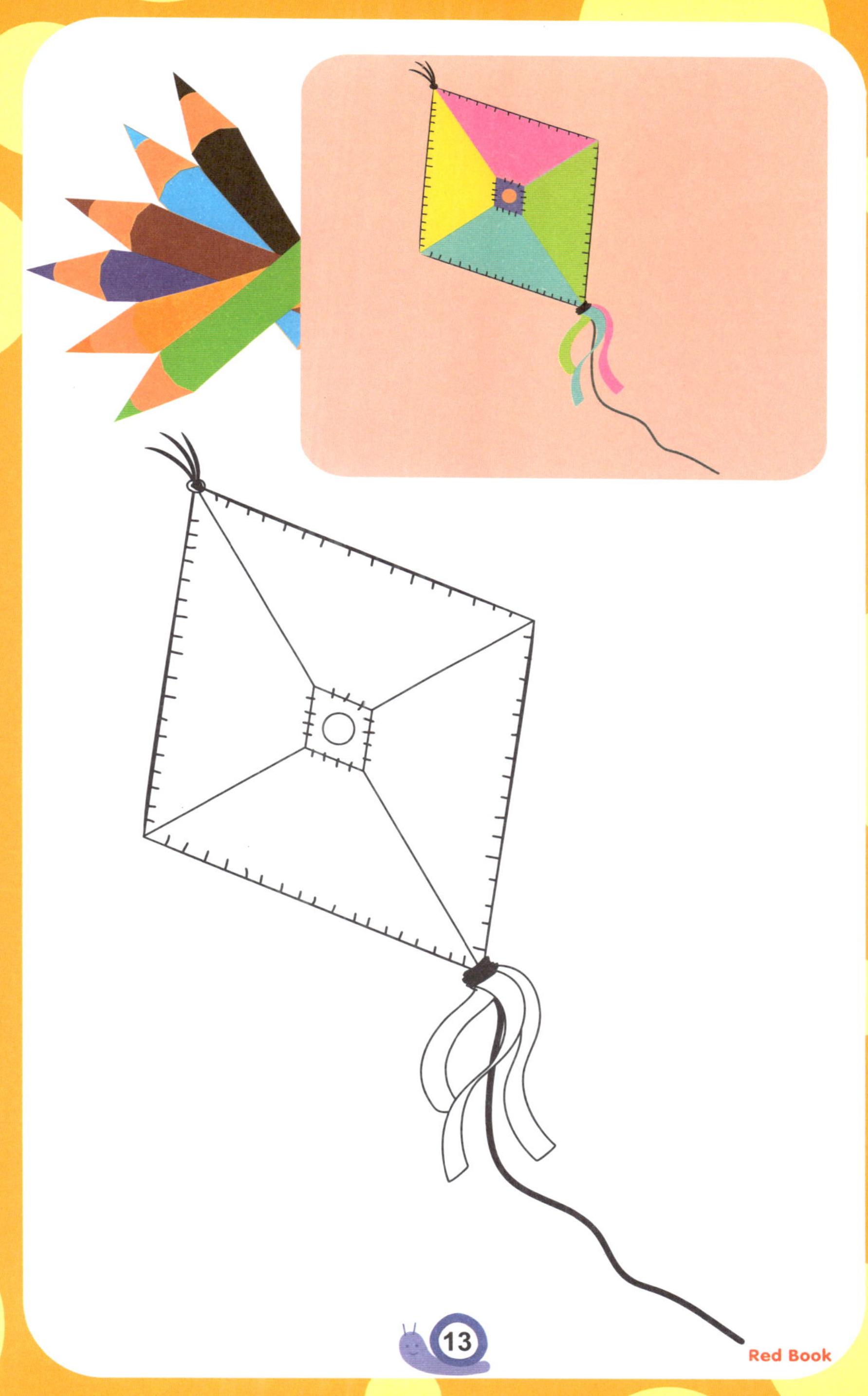

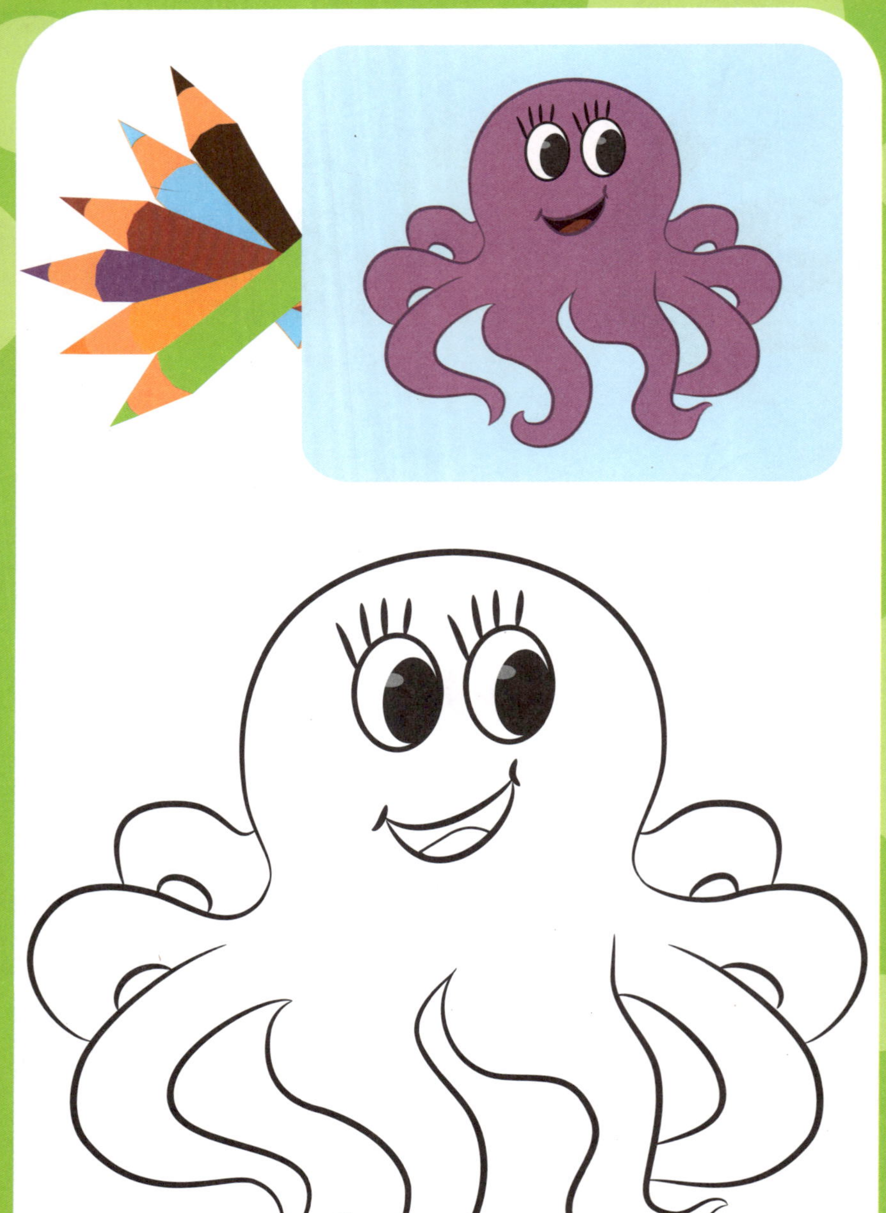

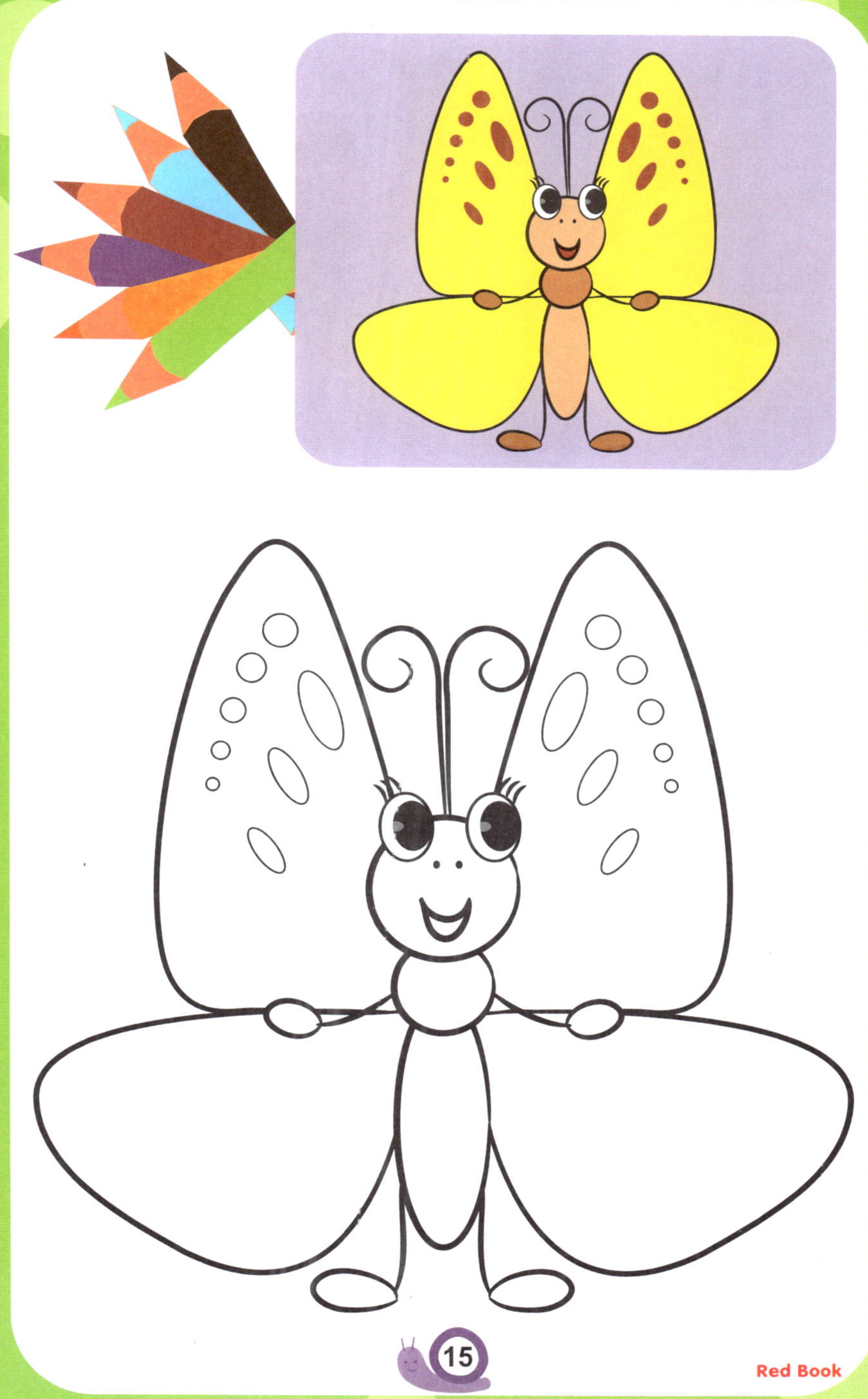

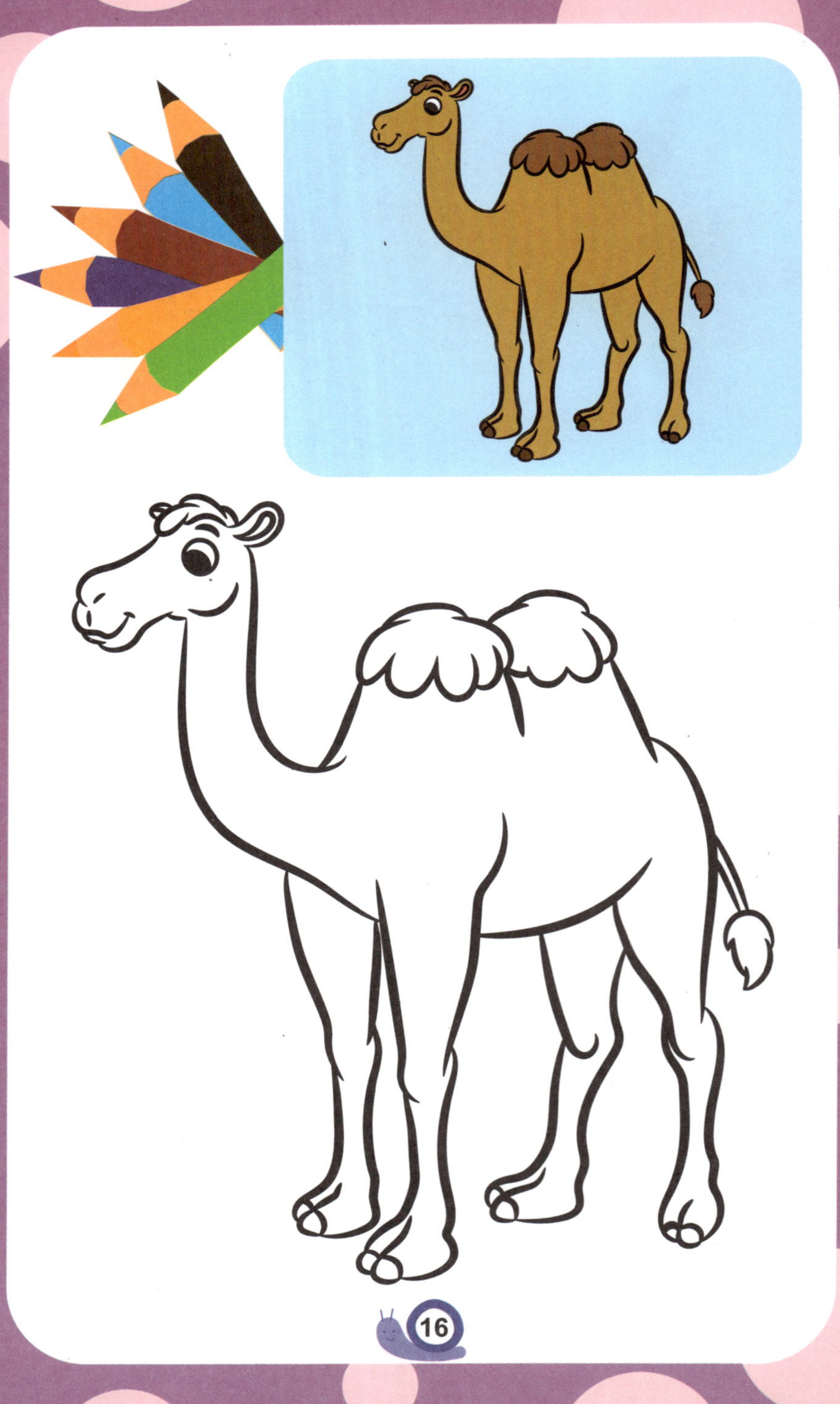